ADVANCE PRAISE FOR BE WARY OF THE ELDERLY

"Poignant, wistful, witty, in love with language play, and with the formal beauty of rhyming, Allan Appel invites the reader into enigmatic and paradoxical realms. With a dramatist's gift running through his lines, and with the disturbance of normal prose syntax, he liberates his poems to make their meaning of pain, hunger, impoverishment and yearning."

Marc Kaminsky, author of *The Stones of Lifta*

"In his new poetry collection, *Be Wary of the Elderly*, Allan Appel takes on big themes—death, old age, plague, the Holocaust—but always with an eye to the personal. His large subjects are meaningful to the reader because they are concrete and palpable. Honed to an ironic edge, sometimes outright funny, but always with deep empathy, these poems reveal the tragedy of the human condition at its most grandiose and also at its most mundane."

Judith Liebmann, author of *Ekphrasis*,
and Poet Laureate of Branford, Connecticut

"*Be Wary of the Elderly* offers dark and sardonic portraits of complex family history and dynamics, the pandemic, being husband, parent, grandparent. Aging and mortality make frequent appearances hovering over a collection of mordant yet whimsical wit. 'Superhero Sonnet' will shake any sentient reader to the core!"

Melanie Greenhouse, author of *Republic of Sunlight*

Be Wary
of the Elderly

ALLAN APPEL

Be Wary of *the* Elderly

POEMS

Finishing Line Press
Georgetown, Kentucky

Copyright © 2025 by Allan Appel

ISBN 979-8-89990-115-7 First Edition

All rights reserved under International and Pan-American Copyright Conventions. No part of this book may be reproduced in any manner whatsoever without written permission from the publisher, except in the case of brief quotations embodied in critical articles and reviews.

Publisher: Leah Huete de Maines
Editor: Christen Kincaid
Cover and text design by Sophie Appel
Order online: www.finishinglinepress.com
Also available on amazon.com

Author inquiries and mail orders:
Finishing Line Press
PO Box 1626
Georgetown, Kentucky 40324

In memory of Janet Abramowicz and Iris Rifkin-Gainer, who have left the stage, and in honor of and delight in Sam, Gabby, Taylor, Annie, McKay, Sadie, Jane, Edie, Posy, Ari, Max, and Theo, who are stepping on.

CONTENTS

A (Pandemic) Preface   ix
Acknowledgments   xi

Assignment   3
Six Green Chairs   4
Ukrainian Dream   7
The Consolation of Philosophy   9
History of the Jews of Los Angeles   12
Encyclopedia Man   13
Jews Are Always in Season   15
The Russia Hotel   16
Vaccination Sonnet   17
Ukrainian Dream #2   18
Suffering's Limit   20
Poem for the Sun   21
The True Miss Universe Contest   22
Pre-Planning for Atonement   23
Superhero Sonnet   26
Raking Season Sonnet   27
Medics of the Night   28
We Lost Joel   29
Dover Beach Redux Sonnet   30
Five Minutes with New Grandchild   31
What Did You Do in the Pandemic, Grandpa?   32
Road Work   34
Auden Redux Sonnet   35

The Grill	36
News Hour	37
Cafeteria	38
The Astronomer	39
The Cleaning Lady	40
Two Bathroom Poems	41
At a Stop & Shop in New Haven	42
Coming to Your Neighborhood	43
Kaddish Sonnet for an Artist	44
Zoom Theophany	45
Be Wary of the Elderly	46
Silence the Rooster	48
Dead Jews at Normandy Sonnet	49
Era of the Apocalyptacene	50
How Allen Ginsberg and James Baldwin Saved Us from Omicron	51
Not the Drowning Side	52
God Riding His Power Mower	54
Proud To Be an Animal	55
Day After Christmas 2022	56
Hidden Pictures	57
Hope Serves Dishonestly	59
Leonard Cohen Move Over	60
Virtue Cannibal	61
Her Perfect Game	62
After Cheating Sonnet, with Two Lines To Go	64
Spying on Mom	65
The Day After the Day of Atonement	66

A (PANDEMIC) PREFACE

A good number of these poems emerged from a place where none of us had ever been prior to 2020—in the midst of the COVID-19 pandemic. At that time I was anointed to be the "pandemic poet" of the *New Haven Independent*, the hyperlocal newspaper or news site where I have been working for now close to two decades.

A shooting, a fire, an aldermanic meeting, a block party, the latest Board of Ed reading statistics, then, thank God, an art exhibition to offset last night's board of zoning appeals talkathon; then the governor buying a cookie at our newest bakery, which had just received a façade repair grant from the state; the funeral of a community leader, even interviewing the splendid horse that pulled the wagon around the New Haven Green at holiday time—these had been my assignments. But never an assignment to be the pandemic poet. Thus the first poem in the collection, "Assignment."

But how do you become this most unusual phenomenon: a temporary public poet—what was that?—and a public poet who also had an actual publishing deadline. My assignment was to write approximately once a week about all the pandemic headlines that don't make the paper, that is, the interior life of all of us who lived through those anxious years.

But how to write for yourself *and* for others? How to be true to the quirky self and also be relevant to my new public? I remember thinking, Hey, we need hospital beds, ventilators, vaccines, not poetry! At first I didn't quite know where to begin, how to find the well out of which useful work might emerge. I felt by turns lost, liberated, and constricted, and even at times under scrutiny by the Independent's often cranky and politically-minded, not pantoum-minded, readers.

Ah well, after a while I believe I found my way, in no small part taking inspiration from writers I admired who also had become, for parts of their careers, albeit on a far grander stage, public poets—writers such as W. H.

Auden and Allen Ginsberg. And so special thanks to them and also to the *New Haven Independent* and a deep bow of gratitude also to my colleague and friend Paul Bass, not only a fine editor but an eclectic reader who believes that anything, simply by virtue of its having happened, qualifies as news, even poetry. Let's hope the news is good.

ACKNOWLEDGMENTS

Some of these poems—a number in earlier versions—have previously appeared in *BoomerLitMag, Connecticut River Review, Deronda Review, Extensions, Fig Tree Lit, The New Haven Independent, New York Times: A Magazine of Poetry, Response, The South Dakota Review, The Whole Megillah, Yellow Mama*, and in Allan Appel's collections, *New Listings* (Horizon/Inwood Press, 1974) and *Not So Much Love of Flowers* (Coffee House Press/Toothpaste Press, 1975).

Be Wary *of the* Elderly

Assignment

I am a reporter and my beat is eternity
Every day something happens that must be covered
When nothing happens, reporters go there too
And give equal attention, it's what we do
That's the challenge, to cover the territory
To double-check tips with our limited staff
Is it not what you expect, what you ask?
Speakers must be accurately quoted
No paraphrases permitted, no surmises
Nothing anonymous, no mistakes or surprises
Not when the stakes are always so high
Nothing buried, or off center, nothing dangling
With eternity it's fact, fact, fact, just the truth
I think you already knew exactly what we do
You've been at it since you were born too
Since you first emerged dazzled and cried
Like it or not we are subscribed
Full team coverage, every second, every breath
Now what might be the angle on your death?
Sure, it's endless and deadlines are tight
Take my number, call absolutely any time
Please, we can do it, let's get our story right.

Six Green Chairs

Six chairs sitting on the wet green lawn
Always makes me feel hopeful
That people are coming, that a call was sent out
And thus seating has been prepared
For the arrival of the six
I never know if they will enter together as a group
And each stand before his or her chair and wait
Patiently, even with a touch of nerves, for the others to be seated
For the chairs are all equal, equally comfortable
Identically built Adirondack chairs, each deep hunter green
And all facing each other over a green oval
Of lawn, a kind of carpet between and before them.
So when these counselors or visitors or
Whoever they turn out to be, whenever one speaks
All can easily take in what the speaker has said
That is, the spacing between chairs is such
You might even call it intimate though no touching will be allowed
The aim being to promote for me a kind of
Neutral thoughtfulness and advice, steady counsel
Of the kind I need right now here on the porch
Where I am surveying the arrangements.
Now if they arrive to sit on my six green chairs separately
Appearing one by one, as I think will be the case,
Each can sit anywhere, for as I've emphasized
All the chairs are exactly alike on the green lawn
I don't know quite why it is so important
That the chairs be identical, for clearly

BE WARY OF THE ELDERLY

I don't want the six arrivals to be identical
To be cut from the same mold, to say the same old things
I need them in fact to have six different views
About my life, the choices I will make today
And in the days to come, whom I will love
And whom I will shun, who help, who ignore
Even if I live or die, a choice, if you think about it,
That is operational on the biomechanical level
Second to second, moment to moment, well, of course
So much is at stake, so much is to be discussed
A diversity of views seems to me critical
If any approach, consensus, or even useful
Advice or direction will be forthcoming.
Once I had seven chairs gathering
But one fell apart, the one now in the shed
But that's okay, an odd number wasn't needed
As a vote was never meant to be taken
And the six look just right, actually quite perfect
Six chairs, maybe like the ones used originally
For a brief rest after each day of creation?
Where a little catnap, a snooze after daily exertions
Was taken before the official day of rest, and why not?
Just because we don't know about it
Doesn't mean it didn't happen
After all it's so beautiful out here this morning
As if right toward the end of the first day of it all
So much glistening, and fresh, so much to be coordinated
That's why this morning's gathering is so critical
Why the chairs must be set up just so
A hodgepodge of different chairs, an old rocker
Or the broken-armed one that could be dragged in
From the shed, those would be no good at all

For all the reasons I've explained
They would diminish the effort that needs to be made
One mismatched or unmatched choice could
Threaten the hope their presence brings
And that is why the six green chairs sit
On the wet green lawn this morning
In their patient circle, waiting, along with me.

Ukrainian Dream

A woman no longer young, not yet old
A woman remote yet also so familiar
Hunched over a brown burlap bag
The bag like the field is brown, worn
The dirt beneath, if it could speak
Would cry, give me some rest, I'm so tired
Have I not done so much, kept you alive
Yes, but barely, yes, mutters the woman
Who is my mother, I believe
From a small town outside of Kyiv
She only once uttered the name, and I forgot
Now she lifts the sack to go, but maybe not
Laboring beneath it she does begin to move
And I am in the sack, I and her dreams
And her worries, which always weigh more than dreams
I'd like to leap out, race across the field
Make my way to Toronto, then cross the border
Illegally to Chicago, I'd like to do all that
On my own, without being a burden to her
But I can't, I'm not born yet
I am still stuck in her sack in Ukraine
And I can't get out, she's keeping me there
I am a Jew, she says, and Ukrainians will spit
On me if I leap out, stay put, she mutters
Stay in the sack, or they will go phew, phew
Spit, spit, the Ukrainians more Nazi than the Nazis
Who rounded us up, who guarded us and handed us

To the Germans to be shot, Ukrainians who now
Have elected a Jew and a comedian their president
If this is not one of the great Jewish jokes of all time
My mother declares, tell me another one and tell it fast
What else do you have in your sack, Mother, I can only ask
Where are you trudging? Back to the village without a name?
Through the dark forest, it is such a long way and I
Am a burden to you, I can see, even in death you are not free
So set us down together, you and I, rest over there
Where the field descends and meets the sky
Where the grass rises leisurely into the future,
Set us down, Mother, before the land begins to quake
Let us out, Mother, both of us, let us wake.

The Consolation of Philosophy

There is some comfort in drugs
And some comfort in sex
And some comfort in art
But there is no comfort
Like the consolation of philosophy
Like the knowledge
That the ship of life is loaded
With its male and female
Of every species and is always moving
Confidently out of the harbor.

There is some comfort
In *The Last of the Mohicans*
Where Uncas son of Chingachgook
Is captured by the Hurons
And tied to a post.
The Huron chiefs jeer at him
And revile him but soon
He turns on them a gaze
Of the most utter contempt:
"Your men are squaws
And your squaws are owls," he tells them.
Then he spits at their feet.

There's some comfort in this
But not like the consolation
Of philosophy, which teaches
You should not look too far ahead
Into your own glory.

There's some comfort in being in love
And some comfort in being alone
In riding the subway late at night
With no one there and no place to go
Hurtling through the dark tunnels
Lights flashing on the dusty windows:
La vía del tren subterráneo
Es peligrosa. No salga afuera
Jesus, Mary, I love you, save souls.

Some comfort here but still the knowledge
Philosophy's knowledge
That no one can say, "You die and I
Take your life into my living head."

I see the consolation of philosophy now
Huge and freshly painted
Rocking serenely as Atlantic rollers
Come bearing in high and strong
From northern seas. As the land buckles
As the rivers turn in their course
As the hills race like young rams
As mares gallop down poison highways
As the hoop snakes put their tails in their mouths
And wheel down the dusty country roads.

The consolation of philosophy
Is gently rocking
With every spokesman's distinction
With every madman's syllable
With every sentence that takes
Forever to pronounce
With every man who no matter how famous

BE WARY OF THE ELDERLY

When he lived
Is now totally forgotten
For want of a writer.

And the consolation of philosophy
Is also slowly moving out
With all our writings
Which really avail us little
Because they perish
Along with their authors
By the continuance
And obscurity of time.

History of the Jews of Los Angeles

José Calderon who lived in my modest adobe house
Two centuries ago and never dreamed
A synagogue would be built surrounded on three sides
By tall Spanish bayonet in the brown soil
Off El Camino Real and tended by
A hairy Russian, my grandfather.

I see him lying on his side on the porch of sienna tiles
Beneath a painting of Jesus dark as driftwood
Later, through a dent in time, to become my window.

Calderon who is shouting to my grandfather
To saturate the ferns, the ferns
May comprehend that down the street
It is the learned year 1914
Sidewalked only on one side and on the other
The unfamiliar clatter of hooves is confusing him.

My father, also confused, steps onto
The street piled with dust
He turns his browned neck to the scaffolding
Ascribes the voices to the sun and recitations from *cheder*
Where I, born that instant in his brain,
Will also learn and, he swears, have a better life.

Encyclopedia Man

I remember a World Book Encyclopedia
White with mottled, expensive-looking green leather trim
Although it turned out to be hard plastic
Something less durable but that
Didn't keep me from starting at the A's
And absorbing all the world's knowledge
Until, like so many other kids, eventually I stopped
Still in the A's, at "aardvark,"
Actually, I always have remembered
A burrowing nocturnal animal native to Africa
Also an A that I have never gone to
And still have not been, oh Africa
Oh aardvark here at the other end of my life
Although I'd very much like to go
At least I've always spelled it correctly, with the double A
"Aardvark" showed whoever was interested
How very much I already knew about the world
And it was also a funny-sounding word
That I enjoyed saying even to myself
When no one was listening but I marked
The spot in the A volume of "aardvark"
With a large strip of blue lined paper
So my parents would know whenever they passed
The bookcase that their investment was paying off.

Today is my father's birthday, he to whom I looked
For knowledge before the encyclopedia arrived
I knew he had it, he must have it,

Even though he was often unemployed and angry
Still he knew things I didn't know
And well into the alphabet, although it wasn't he
Who signed the pale pink paper at the front door
That day the encyclopedia man came
His white cuffed hand extending it to my mother
Who gave the seven dollars first payment
The man said thank you and gave her envelopes
Where further payments would be put and mailed to him
This man also must have known if not everything
Then a lot about the world, after all he was selling the World Book
I didn't think my mother knew much about the world
She was just my mother and yet she knew enough
To take on my father because money was tight
And the seven dollars every week would have to come
Out of the forty he gave her weekly already hardly enough
No, not nearly enough for groceries because he didn't know
The cost of a quart of milk these days
Or a loaf of bread, so she wasn't about to tell him
How much the World Book cost and I wasn't to either
Although I only knew about the seven dollars at the time
Which seemed like a lot of money, though not the full cost
And on the morning weeks later
When they had their fight about the forty dollars not being enough I wondered
If he had so much knowledge why couldn't he find more money?
That was a question I thought reasonable, and clearly my mother did too
But that's all he said, standing just outside of our
Faded blue front door, already down one step
After their shouting finished and he moved off
Into the world to go to work or wherever it was he went
All those entries beyond "aardvark," all those volumes
And slamming the door behind him.

Jews Are Always in Season

As Jews are always in season licenses are not needed
And there are only occasional limits as to number and size
We at the bureau usually look the other way
As the prey in question is elusive, smart, not easily caught
Conditions, however do apply as the hunting varies
From location to location and the calm should not be lulling
Because they are always out there and often
Closer than you know, very close, dangerously so
All agree, therefore, that some target training is desirable
And in some places even required or opportunities
To bag the big ones, for example, might be lost
And the population will grow dangerously out of control
Weekends, from sunset to sunset, appear to be optimal times
For the hunt, also in early fall, or right before first frost
Usually around Thanksgiving they gather in larger groups
Following the cycles of the moon, so check your gear
Wear something warm and of course mind the weather.

The Russia Hotel

Want to be served by surly waiters
Nothing offered but gruel and water
And a short and brutish life?
Have we got the place for you
Scenic yet also deeply primitive
As even nature here holds back
What did you expect from those
To whom evil was done, a picnic?
A tour of the tank tracks in the glade
While you wear your old uniforms
Of course you may dress up
Stuff yourself in them if you still can
You may wander the borderlands
Step across the rutted path
A different country on either side
Very exciting and the vodka
Is cheap, abundant, effective
And democracy can be toasted
To your heart's content even if
It is mocked and hardly wanted
This hotel is a supreme honoring gesture
It is clean, without bugs of any kind
It accommodates the present
By furnishing you with your past
As to the future, of course it too
Can be ordered up, but is always extra.

Vaccination Sonnet

I saw an old friend walk with cane and stoop
Beneath an inviting basketball hoop
Another peered at me above his mask
His names eluded me, both first and last
Yet he seemed to know where I lived, and wished me well
And I right back to him, for, strange to tell
The whole gymnasium where young people usually play
Was full of ambling, forgetful folks on vaccination day
Backboards folded neatly above, nets still and white as snow
Today the shots were taken down below
Yet as they monitored, no, *guarded* me in my white folding chair
I could not have been the only one there
Looking for his spot with this, my fervent wish
Pass me the ball, one last arcing shot, one more swish.

Ukrainian Dream #2

My uncle comes to me in a dream
His gaunt 80-year-old Ukrainian face is just right
But he's wearing a sporty Hawaiian shirt
And has the explosive manner of a Bruce Willis,
A savior hurrying to engage a true archenemy
Or at any rate a busy man on a mission
Even though what he is holding belies that:
One of those corrugated carry-out trays
For beverages, fries, and hot dogs
That you get at a baseball game, although this is Ukraine
And he walks right by, not curious why I am leaving,
As if I'm one of the 50,000 at the game and
He needs to get back to his hungry party
Wherever they are and he has not a second
In his long life or this interval even to say hello
Well, this recognition comes after we have passed
Each other like the proverbial ships in the night
Only this is a stadium, old, noisy, garishly lit
Reeking of sausages or is it cooked human flesh
Somewhere in mid-universe
So I stop, whirl about, and confront him
Abe! Uncle Abe, you there, halt, freeze
Your manners are horrible and you've done
An absolutely inexcusable job uncle-ing
The way he belittled his brother, my father,
Not knowing, when he should have,
What damage that has caused us, this uncle

BE WARY OF THE ELDERLY

So pleased with himself in all ways, so eager to return
To his seat in the stands lest he miss something
But there is a war on, uncle, not a game, in Ukraine
Your Ukraine and now mine, no stadium but a cauldron
Don't you see, can't you understand? I wail
And when I'm done, my say-so spent, my rant complete
My grievances deployed, this uncle with the calmness
Of an unflappable angel or god interrupts:
Fine, come visit us at our table, any time
What table? Why the VIP boxes, marvelous view
The Black Sea, the whitecaps on the Sea of Azov
And he turns then toward the light and the sky
At the entryway to his section of the stadium
And I watch him bound up, two, three steps at a time
Like a young man who of all of us has the best chance
To see the game through, to live forever.

Suffering's Limit

As you set out on your journey to the night
When darkness comes and the bed beckons without sleep
Hope you don't overlook the morning light
How it fell on the leaves' marvelous circuitry
So inspiring and yet they needed you but could not ask
For the water, required you to bestir yourself
And you did, we did, as they trusted us, the shoots, the kids
—What choice did they have, so young, so little —
And by afternoon when we were full of energy and of love
For each one and everyone—we love you all, all, all!—
And neither daunted nor overcome, we did not abandon
Them at the brilliance of midday, we were there—
We've stood in these shadows before, we knew
We just knew it, but we were wrong, so wrong
Yellow-taped by the empty school's door we stood
Guns in hand, teams all arrayed
Wondering who has picked them up, the children,
Who or what has swept them away,
Xavier, Jackie, Eliahana, José
Not the saving but the practice had become
The point, the drills, the alarms turning day to night
Deadly games for fun, with imagined friends
Rescuing the dead, not the living, has become the end.

Poem for the Sun

How many times have I told you I have no matches
And I have no change
And I have no time to listen to your religious beliefs
I must hurry down the ramp
I must board my train
How many times have I told you this
And how many times have I stepped aside
Only to feel your breath on my shoulder
As I descend the stairs and how many times
Have I felt the heat of your speeches
On my neck, how many times felt your eye on me
How many times how many times
And yet you keep coming back every morning
At dawn as if nothing has happened between us.

The True Miss Universe Contest

What if Miss Holland were not a *stroopwafel*
Miss Belize not a jaguar trailing jungle vegetation
Or Miss Ukraine not an archangel with sixteen-foot wings
And Miss USA not a glittery moon landing
What if they were physicists, beautiful PhDs all
Modeling their latest research finds,
Miss Holland as a parallel universe
Would appear as a slice in the loaf of Time
Miss Belize in an intensely dark leotard
And flaming wings defines her expertise in black holes
Miss Ukraine, a top mind in star formation,
Struts her dazzling stellar stuff
And Miss USA, the pride of MIT's anti-gravity dept
Enters walking entirely on her hands,
Her stilettos high above, antennae
Aimed into limitless space, symbolizing
The never-ending search for extra-terrestrial life.

Pre-Planning for Atonement

This part really wasn't a dream although maybe it should have been:
"We recently sent you an email, a follow-up, really,
To the one sent way back in late summer in which
You were given the opportunity, an honor, in fact,
To hold a *Toran* on Kol Nidre. We didn't receive a response
So now we're asking if you will please advise if you want
To accept this honor."

Well, as I like honor as well as the next guy
I did a little proofreader's double take about the *Toran*
I was being asked to carry, for surely they meant Tora*h*
I could find no entry for *Toran* in the Jewish Encyclopedia
So now I began to wonder—and this part *was* a daydream although
I wished it real because maybe—just maybe there was something
Startling, amazing, something new under the Jewish sun
Because God knows—are You listening?—we need that
So perhaps I *am* being asked to hold a holy *Toran*
And I surely do not mean a combo of Torah and Koran
Although that's not a bad idea at all . . . I'm talking about
A new real thing, no typo but a Super Torah
A new something-or-other the inventive Jews
Have come up with, a Torah to the n*th* power!
So blazingly insightful it will lead finally to an honest peace
With the Palestinians, preserve democracy, desalinate
The seas, decarbonize the air, and, frankly, who else
Could do this but us?

On the other hand, was I utterly wrong and was
Something very different at play—now this part
Was also a daydream and I really wanted it to remain that way—
Maybe the offer was nefarious, no honor at all but quite the opposite.
Was it perhaps devious, a strategy to single out
A certain type of Jewish person, someone so careless with
Tradition and the facts he actually thinks a *Toran* exists!
Someone so out there, for example, someone just like me
Who actually checked the spelling, so it was maybe no error
That *I* had been selected, the first chosen one, to hold a *Toran*.

And then I advanced it, because isn't that what daydreams
Are for, to imagine Toran-carrying is being offered
Not to me alone but is trending everywhere.
Percolating out there all around the globe
Something indeed radical and new in the Jewish world.
And it must work like this: Each synagogue by a committee
Vote or urgent rabbinical responsa has been asked to choose
One person, a single member they would like both
To honor and –this is the genius part—honor and also
Get rid of through this powerful new tradition
Called *Toran*-carrying, because the recipient
Doesn't' get the Jews and never will and the Jews
Certainly don't get him, and yet neither can let go of
Each other and that explains the creation of this peculiar
New ritual, an honor as well as a showing me to the exit
In a single brilliant move more clever than kicking me upstairs.

So the daydream draws to a close as I'm in synagogue
Beaming yet empty-handed waiting for the presentation
Of my coveted *Toran*, and I am surrounded by several
Others on the dais, other honorees who, however, are

BE WARY OF THE ELDERLY

Already solemnly holding their Tora*h*s, so of course
I can't help myself but begin covetously to search for it
Wherever the rabbi and cantor have hidden my T*oran*
So you can imagine how when I don't find it in the
Ark, beneath the coverlets or behind the curtain I begin
Really to tear the place up searching under chairs
In the prayer book's hidden compartment, everywhere,
In the rabbi's pockets, in the folds of the cantor's robe
I mean I know it hasn't been invented yet, but seriously
Still, ladies and gentlemen, where the hell is it!
I demand my *Toran*! And yet that turns out to be
The point, precisely. for when I awake I stand among you
It is Kol Nidre and *Toran*-carrying has been the necessary
Prep for the seriously austere rituals, the re-enactments
Now unfolding at the beginning of the end of the world.

In any event, I have responded to your email, and we shall see.

Superhero Sonnet

When she saw the child raising the gun
She must have thought, What have we done
Please put it down, she must have thought
You are a child, a very little boy
The gun was shiny, it was not a toy
Were you fed this morning, were you left alone?
Please put it down, it is real, and so am I
Please lower it, I don't want to die
What is it you are trying to end
Oh I promise I will be your friend
Lower it, and everything will be okay
We can make believe, we'll *re*-start the day
The child listened but did not understand
She had to catch the bullet in her hand.

Raking Season Sonnet

Poems for dead friends are accumulating
Like leaves in the yard in late October
Is this Nature's great hidden secret of the Fall
A leaf for each one of us, for one and all?
A leaf for everyone who has lived and died
The precise number on branches beneath the skies
Growing, looking beautiful as long as they can, being
Useful, providing air, signaling where birds might land
And then they drop to the ground, all done
Graceful, slow, without sound, you never know which one—
Is that you, Peter, Janet, Peggy, Jan?
Which leaf among the millions? Where should I stand
To be near them again, to feel all the giving and taking?
This offers solace in this season of our raking.

Medics of the Night

As you emerge from the shelter accept a prayer
You hear the birdsong before the gunners awake
As you close the door on your vehicle and head out
May the click and tire crunch also make you recall
Your mother pulling in from the visit to school
Her face shining with pride on your good report
As you arrive at the front and bend over him
May the wounded man remind you of whom you love
The blood also the color of beets and holiday ornaments
Until you staunch it with bandages white as perfect snow
You saw for the first time halfway up the Urals
And may you take this brother there with you
Should he die in your arms and if the morgue smells
You will know that even this is only temporary
A lull because the bodies are waiting patiently
For the joke that will finally make them laugh again
By then you will have all the colors and textures
And perfumes of the mind that you will need
Your partner in the ambulance leans near you
His disheveled hair tickles as he whispers it, the joke,
And the entire morgue breaks into sudden, raucous laughter
By now, in any situation, the more horrible, alien, and deadly
The more you will prevail, how strong and loving you've become
And you will drive the vehicle to where the war ends.

We Lost Joel

He was once in this house and I went to see his plays
And laughed at his labored puns and afterwards toasted life
And then we went our separate ways
And I mainly stayed in touch with his excellent wife.
An old friend, she said he continued to produce
Despite a host of maladies and a shaking hand
Words, if not for the ages, then at least for us to adduce
That he'd visited here and he was our friend
Then the virus swept in, she wrote, and took his breath away
And, oddly, she was more at peace than I
With my vain words against age and time, with my puny mission
I protested long life should never be considered an underlying condition
No, she said, they called at three a.m.
The ventilator no longer helped, it was the end
We lost Joel, whom I'd wanted to know well
That's why this is a story I had to tell.

Dover Beach Redux Sonnet

There was a time when gazing at the sea
You might have thought deep thoughts, or poetry
Yet now those days are gone, if ever true
The warming sea abides, but not for you
And now I fear her, mother of us all,
A watery veil extends and then we fall
Head over heels and back to where we came
Small comfort there but only one huge shame
To know just what we did, and yet it's done
So irreversible we cannot run
To call for help—from whom!—is as absurd
As fleeing the planet would be for a bird
The purpose of this note, if it is found
A second human act must be more profound.

Five Minutes with New Grandchild
For Gabby

She looked in person so much smaller than in the pictures
Sent from the hospital all red faced and with features
Scrunched up from the questionably happy trauma
She struck us, all seven pounds eight ounces of her
As sausages quite recently knitted together, such a little thing
The roseate arms sticking out of her white swaddling
All awkward, frustrated, nothing any longer at her command
And we wanted to help of course and offer a token
Of reassurance—though even the air is broken—
As if to say, Don't be disappointed where you've landed
It's still fairly beautiful here, this strange place
We wanted to say, That's your funny nose
And it's roughly in the middle of your face
We wanted to make simple, silly observations, whatever arose
That might bring her, and us, some reassurance
Such as outside of the hall there you see that wavy thing
It's called a tree, with green leaves hanging on branches
As we too are hanging on buffeted back and forth
And, no, you can't see the wind, the cold Covid north
Wind blowing, but, oh, it's there all right,
Which is why we could say little of this, or of day or of night
Beholding her in our daughter's arms in the corridor
Tamping down an impulse to approach, settling only to beam
To say hello and goodbye to our new granddaughter
And now hello again from these miles away
During the required two weeks of quarantine.
We hope we succeeded through our welcoming eyes, that was our task
To communicate love through the blue and white surgical mask.

What Did You Do in the Pandemic, Grandpa?

I listened to the birds while lying in bed
Of course they'd been there before
But I'd just never understood what they said
And wasn't it really such a bore?
No, no, occasionally we went out
To the pharmacy, to the store
But you couldn't do much, right?
Well, no, you could volunteer
Give out food, administer a test
We all tried to do our best
But you really sat tight
That's what you said
It was not like other wars
No bombs dropped, nobody hid under the bed
Yes, yes, but weren't there a lot who died?
More than anyone expected, a never-ending tide
Why couldn't you hide behind the rocks and the trees?
I've told you many times how they called
The little spiked buggers "silent enemy"
I remember, Grandpa, I remember
And what was our main task?
Every day you had to wear a mask
You know where they are up in the attic
Yes, Grandpa, in that old box marked "Pandemic"
And in the beginning it was very tough
You were afraid, right, of every sneeze and cough
That meant it had entered, it had got inside

BE WARY OF THE ELDERLY

It meant there was a good chance we all could die
But that didn't happen and that's why there's a you
Keep talking, Grandpa, tell me some more
Tell me what you did, tell me what's true.
Well, son, it was ordinary, some bad, some good
Like back at the start when Grandma cut out all those hearts?
Yes, and placed them in the windows
A lot of what we did was just give thanks
To the drivers and clerks, the doctors and nurses
To the scientists, of course, to everyone in the ranks
Who finally helped to beat it.
And over the years we've just accepted our fate
It's an art, child, to learn how to wait.
But if we beat it, if we won
Why can't I go outdoors and have some fun?
I'm tired child, and that's what you always ask
Why not go up and just play with a mask?

Road Work

There are always people moving down a road
Dusty or paved, by deserts and trees
There's always a road if there's a need
It begins in one place and through winter and spring
Moves in the direction someone is going
That road we're on, you and I
Is it the same when we close our eyes
When I grow weary and can't go on
When I have to lay myself down
Where will you be then, my friend
Still walking on the road that does not end
Way far ahead, you but a speck yet singing your song
What more can you do to bring us along
Or will you be kneeling here by my side
Clasping a hand while I behold you and die
Then on you can walk for one or for two
That's the secret, isn't it, and I hardly knew
When the night led into the day
When the curve became the straightaway
When here became there, at every turn and fold
We are still together, any steps we take are the road.

Auden Redux Sonnet

We share the sky and the darkening air
We even sometimes speak of our despair
Our sighs and murmurs cover up what's true
That we will always be not one but two
Even thrown together, safely in our shelter
I'm bothered by your ways, you by the welter
Of all my frantic needs and unsaid wishes
I by your messes, you by unwashed dishes
Yet if we wish the present state would end
If only yearning for a truer friend
We come to see that frightens us as well
And that's the tale pandemics have to tell
Auden wrote: We must love one another or die
He forgot to add: At best we can only try.

The Grill

Inspired by Jan Palach in the burning 1960s

I too once considered self-immolation
Yet I knew instantly what a copycat I was
And vain, my problems being nothing like his
Now I'm once again unsure—the killing
Cold in Ukraine and it drones on
The hopelessness in Gaza, it grinds on
Yet what's the point of another burning body
If there are already so many, the sweetish aroma
Of burning flesh so common on the daily grill
And we are all doused in the fine gasoline
Of our endless, unquenchable desires?

News Hour

Tell me more about this news hour
These sixty minutes that rivet your eyes
That I would want to look my way.
Another exploded car
The death of thousands
From flood, famine, disease.
These you loved more than me?
Embarrassed, I kept silent for years
Then one night, as the wine glasses
Finally began to tremble in our hands
I mustered the guilty courage:
Has the power of your gaze
Knitted those body parts together yet?
Flattened those poor bloated stomachs?
Driven away flies from the babies' mouths?
Yet its absence has killed me this very night.
Then die, you said, without looking
Away from the screen and the flame.
Die right here, beside me.
This chair is comfortable
The night is long, the bottle is full
And there will be much news
To ponder before morning.

Cafeteria

Of the lives available, please take one.
Of the deaths offered today, also select one.
Today's specials include happiness, satisfying work,
Identity, love. Of these you may choose one.
Do not crowd. Stay in line.
Dessert is available but not recommended.
Your name is, Today's date is.
Be prepared to pay.

The Astronomer

Although accustomed to wonders
The astronomer trembles
His fingers move uncertainly at the instruments
He puts his eye to the telescope
A satellite the size of our moon looms into view
Its surface strewn with cheap white lawn chairs
The tags still visible: Ikea, Lowe's,
Home Depot indeed.
Around them are concentric circles
Gleaming mounds of crushed metal.
Possibly tin cans? Nearby another celestial body approaches
An asteroid, perhaps of frozen wine, its tail on fire
And there, most peculiar, a planet ringed entirely,
So the spectroscopy immediately confirms,
By clouds of human bone dust.
Yes, we are not alone, but perhaps we should be.

The Cleaning Lady

To run down the same three streets forever
Omniscient crows overhead
And the cleaning lady changing numbers on the door.
A painter is retouching smoke
Rising from the inn where I thought a curve began
But there is only a troupe of players
Smiling at the cul de sac.

To run and run into the evening of an early century
Fence posts racing by like spent heroes
The glass is in your face from objects
Breaking in the mirror far ahead.

Two Bathroom Poems

Washing Up

Among the pipes there is one drop of water
Slowly making its way with the rest
I hear its voice clear and strong
In the silence of the pipes:
Don't let me be the one, it says,
To come up last at the mouth of the faucet
When you finish shaving in the morning.
Don't let me be the one to be caught last
When you finish washing at night.
I am so tired and I can't stick any longer
Don't let me be the one to go it alone
The porcelain is so hard
And such a long drop away.

Porcelain

I will clean this porcelain tub
Until it shines like prizewinning teeth
I will dust and wash this floor
Until it is alabaster under my feet
I will wash this window
Until it sees through the air.
I will work cleaning into a metaphysics
Until I have dispatched everything behind
And only the future remains for me
To scrub with soap and warm water.

At a Stop & Shop in New Haven

Donning mask, gloves, and baseball cap
Like a thief I go out to shop
No surprise everyone's dressed like that
It's kind of fun to see all the robbers by the Cheerios
And that gaggle of felons
Keeping distance by the melons
But now in comes a fellow with no gear at all
Healthy-looking, asymptomatic, and tall
The store grows quiet, then with a start
The thieves scurry off with their wiped-down carts
This man's stride is sure, his smile long and bright
He's the one likely to take your life.

Coming to Your Neighborhood

I vowed to run around every monument
In every continent and country
Every plaque, statue, and memorial
One circumambulation in silence
At every place of holocaust.
Hearing only the thwack of my sneakers
Or birds if they happened still to be about.
Occasionally school children will peer at me
Tourists look up from their guides.
Only once a guard stopped me.
Show some respect, he said.
And he was right. I've run around hundreds
And even here, in this place of bones, my concentration lags
And it's my own children I think of.
These trying children who say
Why are you doing this?
Yet who will throw their arms around me
When I return and kiss me
With their sweet red mouths
Saying, Daddy, My Daddy, You're my Daddy.
Until they arrived, no one ever called me that.
When they depart, no one else ever will.
Do you understand me now? Feet on dirt
The breathlessness of it, I tried to explain.
The heart. The pounding in the temple.

Kaddish Sonnet for an Artist

For Janet Abramowicz

You asked me to say for you the mourner's prayer
But to give it a twist, something fresh but also grayer
So all right, here we go. Have you truly left your studio
Are you already aloft, and where did you go
Are you en route to the water, to the bay
Are you now etched into the plates of the day?
Are there other ways to summon, draw you near?
To hear your irony, sharp, sweet, and dear?
You who knew us so well and are now detained
In a zone or a realm where little is explained
Even this memory, this evoking you tonight
What is it but a flicker of God's energy and light?
Please receive our thought, may it do its part
To renew us, which was your art.

Zoom Theophany

You're in my gallery view here in the darkening room
Where you made regular appearances long before Zoom
And it's confused me about the here and now
And it's raised deep doubts about where we go
When we turn off the sound and the video
How many times have you waved to me from over there
Like a contestant on Hollywood Squares?
You smile, you smoke, your hazel eyes are bright
Is it really you, my companion, on these fitful nights
Who says so little yet looks so right
And your background never changes, I especially like that
You never raise your hand and you never chat
Yet who else can sense my every thought
No matter how fanciful or overwrought
Dare I conclude that death may be only fleeting
And I will see you again when I rejoin the meeting?

Be Wary of the Elderly

I've always been intrigued by the elderly
Though I've never liked the word
Too fragile and lyrical for the harder truth
Their manner no longer thrashing
And competing, more akin to material things
Quiet like the chairs and tables around them
The stones in the garden, trees on the street
Very solid. They just seemed to fit in more
And if I reached my hand out to them
They would tell me, they might not speak
They might not use words yet somehow
They would give me access and for certain
I would discover this secret—
I never really had a name for it —
Although something solid I sensed.
And how badly I wanted it
To be that way *before* I grew old
To get a head start on that . . . whatever it was.
But a problem has arisen
Now that I too am old: I'm not like them at all
I'm a grouchy, cranky, complaining,
Miserable, difficult, meteoric human being
Having expended my elderly contentment
Far too soon when I was younger
I'm full of aches and pains
I eventually "share" with everyone like it or not
And every season for me

Has become one of discontent
Though I try to rediscover
That thing that I craved and even
Possessed, however briefly, decades ago.
So there it is, if you come to visit, if you're
Friends of my children or friends
Of their friends and if you happen
To be dropping by, don't believe what you see
My smile might be pleasant, but, sorry to report,
It conceals, and that's just the way it is, I guess—
As for anything I might say that's wise
Chalk that up to an after-effect of medication.
Or likely something else even more threatening
And if you too are fond of the elderly
Be careful how close you get to us
We're dangerous, we'll really do almost anything
To have what you possess in abundance
And squander it, as we of course did too
So there it is…… I was always fond of the elderly
And now you know
However, if you still care to visit
Mornings are best, and on bright days if possible
Because the danger grows with the onset of darkness
As the day turns and the old face the night.

Silence the Rooster

Silence the rooster, kill the dead
Remembering, we forget ourselves
Even as we go after that fowl
Especially as we do in the liminal time
As night turns to day, it's critical, even sublime
To get your hands around that bird and to squeeze
Out the good light and the bad onto the morning breeze
Yet the creature's always gone, an absence stone hard
And there's always only an empty yard
Yet with coops, bowls, and bins overturned
As if the struggle has already played out
Yet you were not present, you were AWOL
And the consequence is enormous, an abyss, a fall
To where, nearby, on the green expanse
The blades of grass begin to advance
It is happening yet again, the rising, the stir
What you've always hoped for you may infer
This morning, every morning that begins with a dawn
As the dead stretch and gather on the lawn
And now want to see if we can show them
Something, anything they don't know already
Speak to them of this good day, and remain steady.

Dead Jews at Normandy Sonnet

The cemeteries stretched above the sea
Crosses and stars speaking of what they know
And I tried to catch it, the chorus, row upon row
It wasn't the crosses somehow speaking, no by far
The voices I heard most clearly came from the stars
And why was it I admired so much the Jews who were dead?
I hadn't been born, had they died for me instead?
More troubling yet, why did I admire them so much
While with the living Jews I'm so out of touch?
Maybe it would be better to rake the field clean
Secular white plaques for all the way to go
Let God complain, who else need know
Would that be more moving, or would that be less?
And would the dead say we have passed their test?

Era of the Apocalyptacene

Here we are again on the margin of vanishing lakes, in the cold eye of thundering squalls, as if the Noahide flood is debuting its fatal return performance. And so it goes, this new era of the apocalypse everywhere, generating what kind of behavior? You'd think Nero-esque self indulgence but that's not the case at all. The peculiar quality of the Apocalyptacene is in its way of being slow, thoughtful, even gracious, as if we are all newly appreciative of science's methodical, research-solid invitation to the funeral; as if we are actually surprise attendees at the funeral rites, politely offering our seat, stepping aside for someone less firm on their feet . . . yes, death is firmly in the room. But so is . . . what? A desire for the metaphorical orchestra to play on while we play out, while we march on. We check our face in the mirror, our collective compound face as if we've already evolutionarily regressed. For we are both the important guest and also the corpse-in-training. In this as in everything else, there's less new than we think. Religious orders used to march through the medieval streets dressed as skeletons, bearing skulls, to remind the lazy or irreverent of the unavoidable to come. Music, song, sticks clacking on smooth bone, the *danse macabre* emerges. And so we sign off once again with this happy reminder: Brush your teeth well every day, for after your flesh has turned to dust, your marvelous choppers, with their natural hardness second only to diamonds, will remain and future children well might dig you up years hence when they are at play in their dusty bone yard. Yes, there you are, immortality. So let's at least start them out with a smile.

How Allen Ginsberg and James Baldwin Saved Us from Omicron

To drive Omicron away, to sleep without fever dreams
To curl up inside the curves of the letters
To dream in Greek, to become one with the swerve
Remember the beginning *was* in words
In syllables and sounds, the Om Om Om
So to jettison the others, the "i" and the "cron"
Is how we keep from breaking down
So would think saintly Allen Ginsberg
And impish James Baldwin and how, yes,
They would exchange their state
To be right here with us, to share our fate
Back here on this infected planet
Even for a day, a minute, an hour
They knew how to deal with sorrow
They knew how to take a curse
And turn it into the first sound in the universe
Would Jimmy give up his smoking, sure, you wish!
Would Allen lead us in a national *kaddish*?
No, they'd move right in to preach and chant across the land
Everyone together at the same time, hold hands
Across countries, cultures, alphabets, zones
Chanting Om, Om, Om, bye, omicron, Om Om
Sending out into all the respiring world that sound
Everyone together, in a chorus, in a round
Defang it, repurpose the name, say it, sing it, today
Take back the letter, drive the disease away.

Not the Drowning Side

Of all possible disasters
I think I'd take flood
Though not the drowning side
Only the whooshing flow
The being carried away
Even refreshed, the possibility
Say, of swimming past houses
Lapping cars, there the neighbor's dog
Which you would of course try to help
Then the two of you evade
The whirling deadly debris, of course
All the spinning exciting speed of it
And then suddenly you are washed
Ashore, say, on a pristine island
Searching for survivors
Where new adventures begin
Whereas with fire, avalanche,
Plague and pandemic, tsunami,
Earthquake and Disaster's other
Usual suspects there are,
To my still childish imagination,
Few outs though I grew up
In California where the rainwater
Rising over the high curb
Sherbourne Drive became a river
Grownups wondering aloud
If their Hudsons and Plymouths

BE WARY OF THE ELDERLY

Will be swept away, finding the rope
Tying it on, the bravest one
Not my father, but another
Whom I can't remember but for this
Wading out, trying to open the door
Holding on, to get a purse left
On the back seat, I beside
Someone's pant leg
At the floor-to-ceiling window
Looking, admiring, my heart beating
With the safe peril, the green-brown water
All the gone cars, the gone people
Gone not by flood but by the other one,
By time, these words, the rope
For when the water returns.

God Riding His Power Mower

The vast green lawn in the Garden of Eden
Needed no watering; was perfect and even
As breath is in darkness, in deep, quiet sleep
Until humans arrived and with them the sheep
And the goats, who did the first mowing.
But their work was uneven and very slow going
So He invented teens who at least might know
The parameters of the job, of how to mow.
But He had forgotten how, at His behest
Humans were granted a day of rest.
So what was the Lord God now to do
With the fertile lawn of heaven and no crew
While the earth below now screamed
For vast amounts of water to keep itself green?
So He altered the rules of heaven on the fly
From green to blue so the grass could be sky.
There was little now to do but admire the blue vault
Proof, finally, He had no fault.
And the planet flourished and time sped on
Till God began to miss His lawn
The slant of grassy hillside, the vista, the scent
Of wet grass at sunset, the green meaning of what He meant.
So the water's diverted again and the earth's gone brown
The sky's tinged Eden green, everything's upside down
With God joyriding on His power mower above
We struggle to find more water, and more love.

Proud To Be an Animal

Why is it they kill in such numbers
Their own and eat not even a morsel
Or lap a drop of the salty warm red blood?
Their voices, the *grrr* of their thoughts
As they amble over the rectangular mounds
Murmuring on the refreshing night wind
Their heads up and alert, now down sniffing
And pawing at this scent of human mass death
Familiar yet never so unappealing, even noxious
That they nudge their young, the pads of their feet
Sinking into the still soft dirt, please notice,
Boys and girls, cubs and fledglings
Don't you *ever* become like them!
Be proud to be the animals that you are
Killing when you are hungry
Eating to satisfaction, abjuring waste
Admiring the speed of the herd as it escapes
As this makes you close to the divine
You must pledge never to fall as low as this,
Never strive to be human
But remain what you are, proudly so—
They say, sniffing and ambling over
The last rows of shallow hummocks
Pausing at the final row with its odd crisscross of sticks
Moving on, then with a wary backward glance
Into the dark and welcoming forest.

Day After Christmas 2022

My son told me I was old and it was not as if I hadn't known
Yet there was something in the way he said it
A kind of proof or conclusion offered
A power, a weighty observation and I should have asked
If I had done or said something to merit the new designation
Yet the opportunity escaped and this eats at me,
Through me, it felt so definitive, so irreducible
And here I am lifting an arm to wave goodbye and it hurts
Where it never did before as if goodbye not only to him
But also to a previous version of myself
And he doesn't look or act like me at all
That's the greater mystery, the thrall.

Hidden Pictures

For Sam

You know how the comb serves
As a fence post or gate or railing
That's exactly how to play it
The slice of watermelon beneath the clasp
Of the little girl's purse the pizza slice
That's a wedge in the wheel of the bike
The arrow that masquerades as a flower
You get the idea, a kid's game I play
In the monthly activity book with the child
To pass the time this third day of heavy rain
I'm the grandfather and more and more
I'm believing in hidden pictures
Things not where we should find them
But do, on the couch where we play, the child and I
Look, with no permits needed the gun
Floats already at the daycare center, how clever
It's white and nestled among the diaper supply
I found it! And here's another for me,
Yes! In the tall elegant church candelabrum
Bearing a flame right out of the barrel, blue and orange
Who would have thought, and then, yes, indeed
On the next page among the produce
In the supermarket this time another weapon
And another, shiny and shoulder to shoulder
With the red onions and Japanese eggplants
Alas, they are not hard to find at all
And I turn back to his game, feather in a cloud

Volleyball hanging in the sky, the moon, the moon!
Right there, he cries, right there, sad moon face
Bearing down on the gun-metal gray world below.

Hope Serves Dishonestly

The others write about darkness too
And yet always somehow find light
A star, a streak of pink at dawn, all the
Calling cards hope scatters about
Tempting us to find them, cemeteries
Perhaps with a fallen bouquet, shriveling,
Yet at least it's there, left by a loved one, or trees
Upright on the margins, beautiful in moonlight
Bathing the stones, and on and on the glimmers
Competing for attention like beautiful women
In a contest, proud, erect, heads high
The long legs of hope striding through the storm
Yet even they are soon swept away,
The cleaning crew and janitors arrive
And, having done their job, in turn await their exit
Always my failing, my light always suspect
My light always with stage fright
Dashing away just when its turn has arrived
Just when it is needed most, even when sent by you
But what can I do? Hope serves me dishonestly
If I just drizzle it on like a seasoning
But then I am stuck, as now, with how to end
Without being phony or rude, with how to walk out
Close the door, not slam it, but just click it shut
The way it is, not locked, but always so hard to open.

Leonard Cohen Move Over

And thank you for the space, for allowing a guest
To preside over the long-running show
Of ourselves recently canceled. You see there too
How even the babies are no longer cute as they were
And the unborn also are having trouble finding their audience
And even the dead, as you well know, are no longer
Capable of providing the usual and reliable service.
The ball dropped yet everyone running as if nothing
Has happened, a humiliation so public
And so universal no one notices
Yes, there was nothing new in this
Although it of course felt that way
And now that we have been noticed
We may as well shake our own hand
Again and again, poor dumb creatures
Who don't know the difference
Between congratulation and consolation
We can only wait and hope, whatever that is,
That someone, somewhere—perhaps you—will
Send the right message our way—will see and cry,
Finally! Enough! Enough grief. Let us try again.

Virtue Cannibal

The dead like these holidays too
And yet this batch are all Jews, it seems,
But, no, here, I am relieved, to find others
I can consume, obituary devourer that I am
Their achievements and warm presence,
Their humor and love and courage in the storm
Each life I take, as if from a jar of vitamins, a bowl
Of marvelous chips I savor, chew over, and consume
At first a few, a handful, then there's no stopping
Me as I read, absorb, infuse their traits
Consuming like a kind of cannibal of virtues
A well-crafted portrait of a saintly woman
This marvelous African-American saxophonist
And then somehow the ideal accrues to me
The talents too, I read, I gobble up so that
Finally I can rise from this chair a wiser, kinder
More accomplished, even brilliant person
Perhaps a Nobel winner, which is why, as I take
The paper in hand I note the worthy causes
The charities designated by survivors
I feel a generosity of spirit forming inside me
A new calling that may also be some fun
Which is well, as so much remains to be done.

Her Perfect Game

With the odds against, 46,800 to one
You threw *two* of them, a feat men
Have come near but never achieved
So thank you and may I extend
That on this morning to my wife
Who has just asked me to explain
The difference between a no-hitter
And a perfect game, and it gets even better
When I am able succinctly to say it's a gem
Twenty-seven up and 27 down
No one reaches first base, which is maybe
Not a perfect explanation, perhaps a
No-hitter of an explanation and yet as she
Continues to sit there in the corner
Of the couch, in our little living room
Her legs tucked under her, still athletic and strong
Reading of your feats, I feel I have left out
The business of strike-outs and balls fouled off
And if baseball's definition of perfect games
Should consider pitch-count and strikeouts
But it doesn't although Roger Clemens
Struck out 20 in a non-perfect game
And the record for strikeouts during
A perfect game is 14, and the lowest pitch
Count in a perfect game is 74 out of a total
Of 81 possible (three batters times three

BE WARY OF THE ELDERLY

Times nine innings) but that was in 1908
I would explain to my imperfect wife
If she weren't still reading so slowly
But I bet you came close, Jean, although
They don't list those stats, only saying
You were clearly the greatest of all time
In the All-American Girls Professional
Baseball League, but let's just say
One of yours came close to the truly most perfect
Not only striking out 81, but pitches
So well planned and executed
For you could remember each batter's
Sequence at each rotation, and you varied
It the next time you faced her, and the next.
Just saying, that if anyone could strike out 27
And in a manner that no bat ever touched
Your fast ball that hopped like it was on fire
And no wood ever got near your curve ball
That broke off like a country road,
That person was you, that game was yours
Whiff after whiff so that the ball was
White and unscuffed as a hazy moon
At the end of the game as it was at the beginning,
Has somehow landed here in our stands
Unblemished in our little living room
My wife still reading of your South Bend Blue Sox,
How you mystified the Rockford Peaches,
With only the sound of the newspaper
Rustling, this quiet, peaceful, perfect morning.

After Cheating Sonnet, with Two Lines To Go

All these years after I cheated on the math test
Because I simply didn't understand how
A negative times a negative could ever be positive
I still don't get it, so a friend sent me a tutorial.
Now that I'm old I no longer worry about my grade
Or at least not *that* one, though I am worried about the grave
And I wonder if I should die without understanding . . . what then?
Or if I *do* finally get it, will the Great Negativity close in?
On the other, other hand, to go from negative to plus
Isn't that the direction we strive for, all of us?
And so I go around it, I understand, I don't understand, it's like a dance
We live and we die, mostly, in ignorance.

Spying on Mom

For Marc Kaminsky

I like to stand in the kitchen as my mother used to
A cup of coffee in one hand, and in the other
Something to eat usually bread with butter
A stale piece, something simple even a crust
Often something left by us
Her location varied, sometimes beside the sink
Or in the corner near the cabinet above the red
And white plastic box for bread
Not standing nor leaning neither at rest
Nor poised to leave, a bit like a broom
Without a handle, just there, surveying
Her modest realm, the kitchen and breakfast room
Against the refrigerator, the new Amana—
Which she loved above all, her pride and joy
The one appliance that worked
Amid all the other breakdowns of her life—
Against that gleaming white door
She would never lean; as she hovered through time
It was always in view, its quiet hum, its lovely shine.
Maybe that was the object of her gaze
As she stood there, all the afternoons of her days
Looking and looking, as if for a refuge or a prize
Until I entered the room and met her eyes.

The Day After the Day of Atonement

The day after the Day of Atonement, my darkest day
I felt the universe expanding, driving me away
From everyone I'd known and loved
On a jet—the comparison came to me
But not as passenger, but on the wing
Trying to balance, maybe on the crest of a wave of time
And space relentless, moving, with a sense only of *away*
And no markers anywhere, no destination in sight
A dark, directionless flight
And there in the wake a growing debris trail
Of my loves, poems, papers, shoes and socks
My plate, my bowl, my treaty, my contract
Curling family photos, those of the Holocaust dead
Migrants huddled under the international bridge
Scenes from Seinfeld, ventilators covered with tarps
Toothbrushes—all there in an endless plume behind
As we zoom on and on, not into darkness—
That's not what made the day dire—but into an unknown
That the doctors of comfort call god or home
Or return, but they have their own darkness
And they know little more that we do of it
Which is only this dizzying speed on a vehicle without
Brakes or restraints or windows or aisles or . . .
The language can't keep up with the acceleration, and I
Finally rose in the morning just before light and looked out
I sensed gravity all around like dew on the grass
Doing its level best to hold things down

And the coffee with two marvelous sweet cubes of sugar
All stayed in my cup, so I drank the coffee
The dark, dark brew of the day after the Day of Atonement
And I inhaled and sipped another sip of darkness
And strangely enough, felt happy.

ALSO BY ALLAN APPEL

Poetry

New Listings
Not So Much Love of Flowers

Nonfiction

The Squire of East Hampton
A Walk Through a World of Plants
36 Stories of Memory and Hope
A Portable Apocalypse

Novels

Judah
Vengeance Valley
The Rabbi of Casino Boulevard
High Holiday Sutra
Club Revelation
The Midland Kid
The Hebrew Tutor of Bel Air
The Book of Norman

www.ingramcontent.com/pod-product-compliance
Lightning Source LLC
Chambersburg PA
CBHW030056170426
43197CB00010B/1545